Aa _______

Apple _____

Alligator

____

Ant _____________

The ant ate the apple.

____

The Alligator loves to swim.

____

The apple fell from the tree.

____

Bb________

Banana __________

Bee ________

Bike __________

The Banana is yellow.
____
The Bee loves Honey.
____
The bike is white.
____

Cc _______

Cat _______

Car _______

Carrot _______

The Cat is very Cute.

____

The Car is red.

____

The Carrot is Orange.

____

Dd

Duck _________

Dog _________

Dolphin

____

The Duck Swims in the pond.

____

The Dogs love to play.

____

The Dolphin lives in the sea.

Ee _________

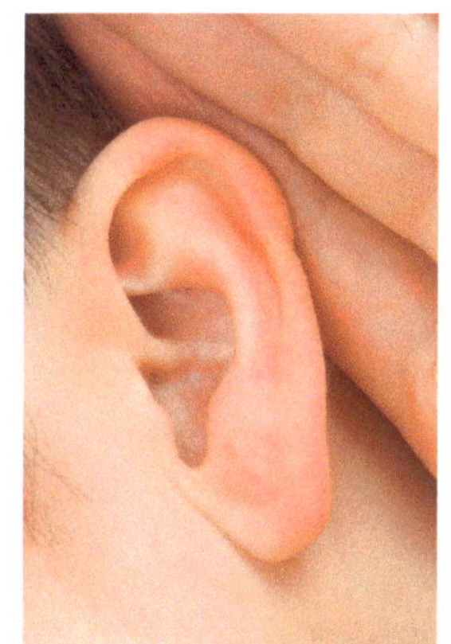

Ear _________

Eye _________

Elephant

____

I can Hear from my ear.

____

I can see from my eyes.

____

The elephant Is very big.

____

Ff _______________

Frog _____________

Flower __________

Fish _______________

The frog loves to jump.

____

The flower is very pretty.

____

The Fish is orange and
white.

____

Gg ___________

Grapes

____

Giraffe ___________

Gift ___________

The Grapes are Purple.

____

The Giraffe is very tall.

____

The Gift has a red bow.

____

Hh _______

Hat _______

Horse

____

Hamster

____

The Hat is red.

____

The Horse loves to run.

____

The Hamster is very small.

____

Ii_________

Ice cream

____

Igloo ___________

Iguana

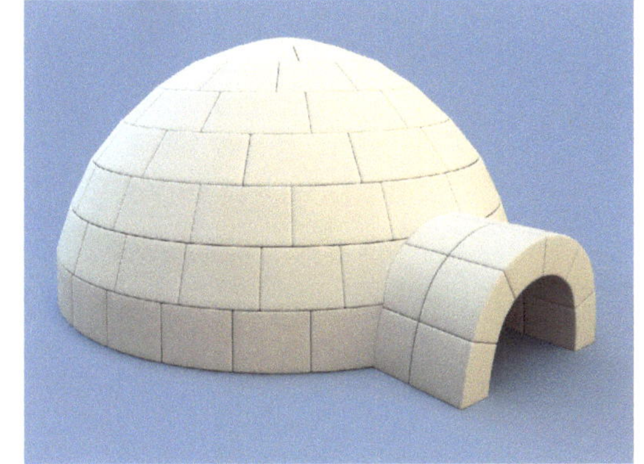

____

The Ice cream is Yummy.

____

The Igloo is very cold.

____

The Iguana is green.

____

Jj __________

Jeans

____

Juice

____

Jacket

____

The jeans are blue.

____

The Juice taste like oranges.

____

The jacket is blue.

____

Kk ______

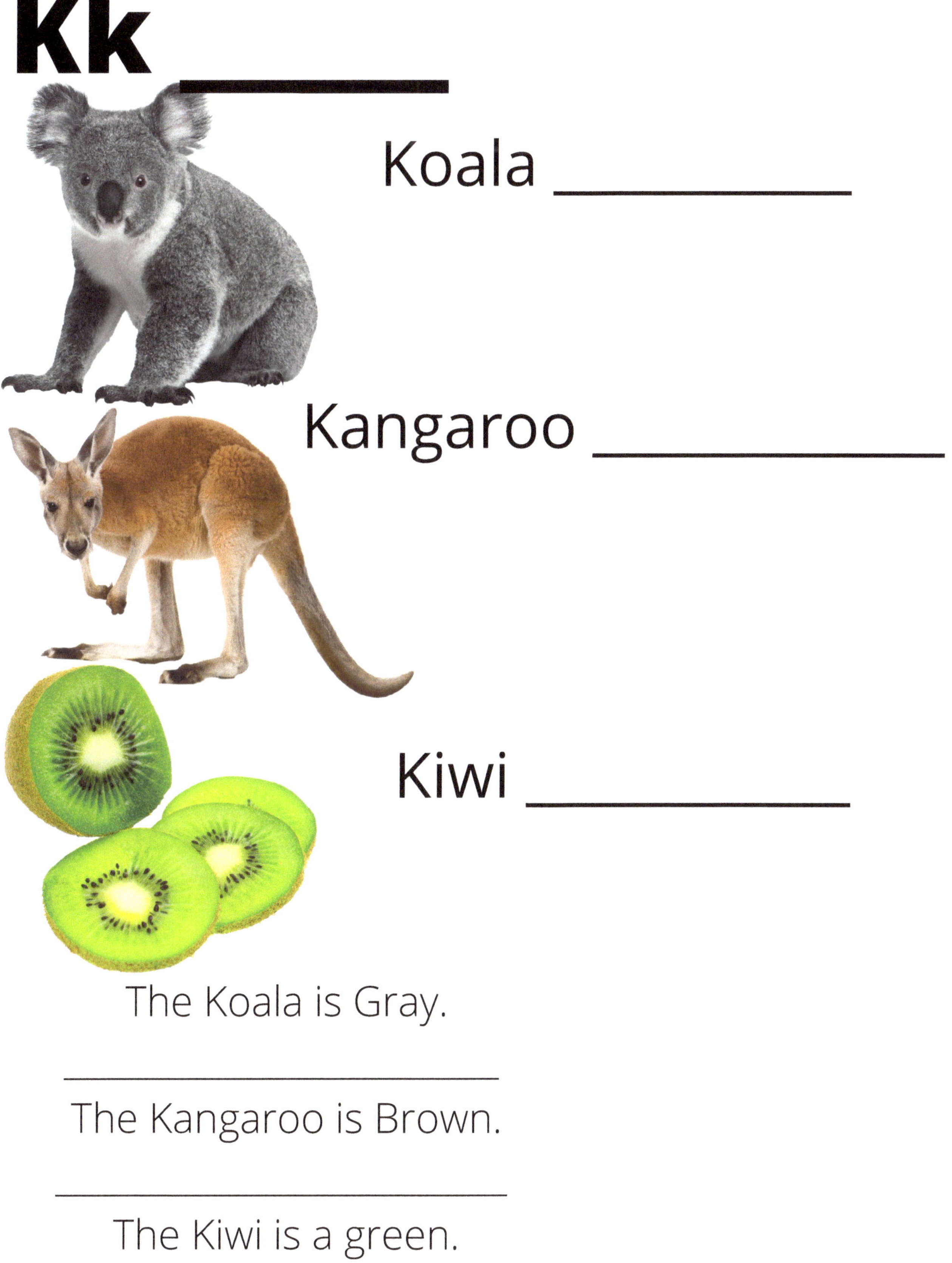

Koala ____________

Kangaroo ____________

Kiwi ____________

The Koala is Gray.

____

The Kangaroo is Brown.

____

The Kiwi is a green.

____

LI

Lion _________

Leaf _________

Lady bug

____

The Lion is the king of the jungle.

____

The Leaf is green.

____

The Lady bug eats leaves.

____

Mm _______

Moth

____

Monkey

____

Moon

____

The Moth is brown.

____

The monkey loves bananas.

____

The moon is full.

____

Nn

Necklace

____

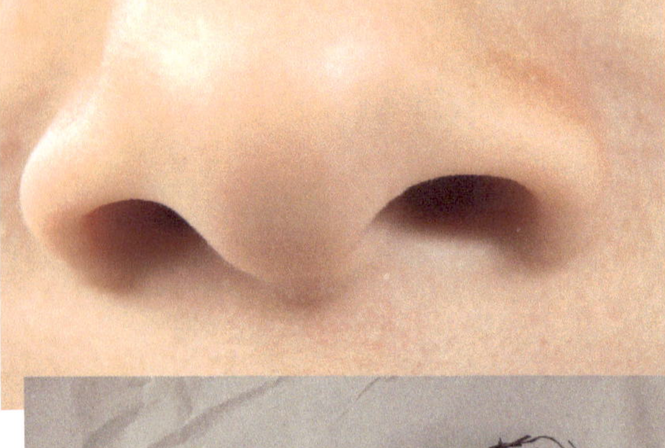

Nose

____

Nest

____

The Necklace is pretty.

____

I can smell with my nose.

____

The birds lays eggs in the nest.

____

Oo

Orange

____

Octopus

____

Otter

____

The orange is healthy.

____

The octopus has 8 legs.

____

The otter is very cute.

____

Pp ________

Pumpkin

____

Pie

____

Pencil

____

The pumpkin is orange.

____

The pie is very delicious.

____

I use my pencil to write.

____

Qq

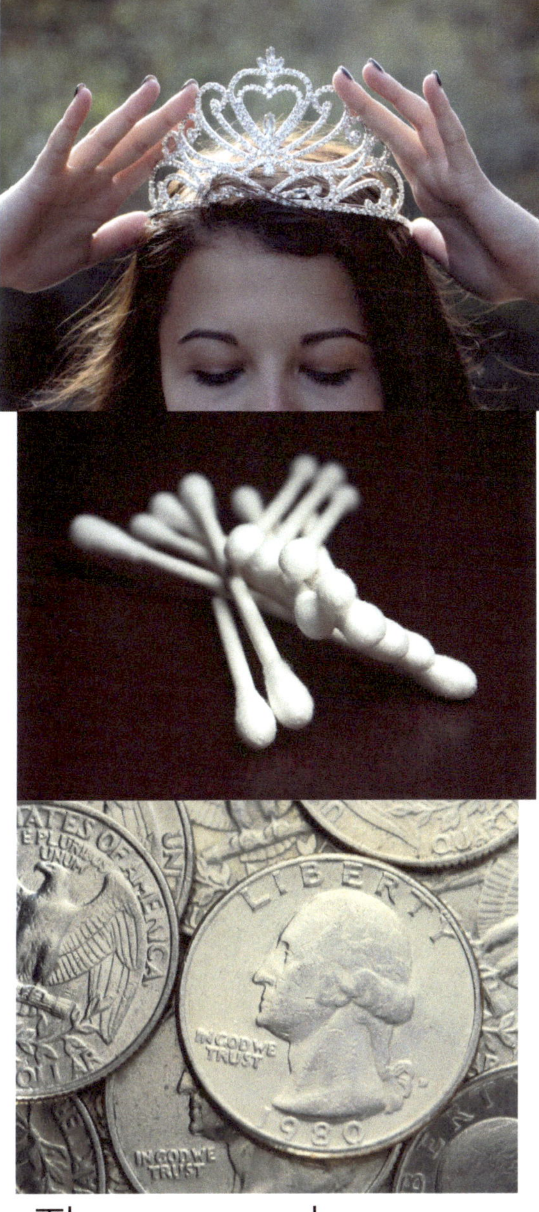

Queen

____

Q-tip

____

Quarter

____

The queen has a crown.
____
The Q-tip cleans the ears.
____
The quarter is sliver.
____

Rr

Rocket

____

Rainbow

____

Rose

____

The rocket goes to space.

____

The rainbow is colorful.

____

The Rose is Red.

____

Ss______

Snake

____

Snowman

____

Spider

____

The snake is smooth.

____

The snowman is cold.

____

The spider has 8 Legs.

____

Tt

Turtle

____

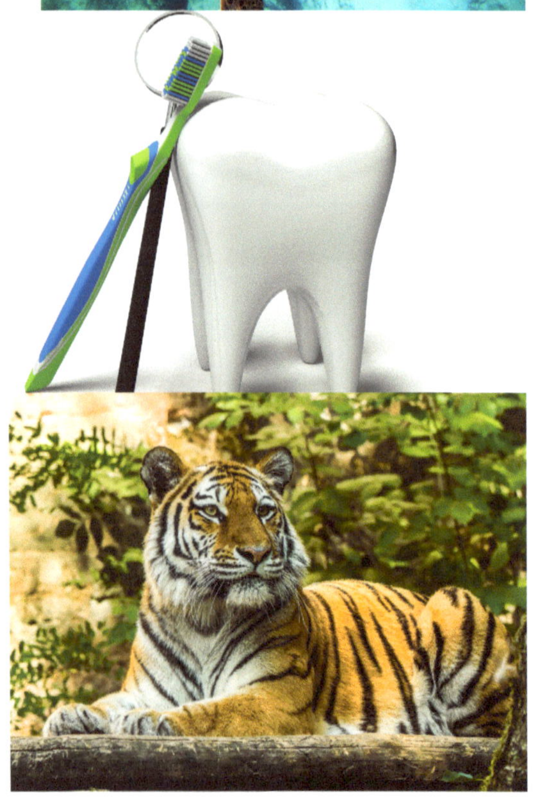

Tooth

____

Tiger

____

The turtle swims.

____

I brush my teeth everyday.

____

The tiger has stripes.

____

Uu

Unbrella

____

Unicycle

____

Unicorn

____

The unbrellas are colorful.

____

The unicycle is fun.

____

The Unicorn is beautiful.

____

Vv

Violin

____

Vase

____

Volcano

____

I can play the Violin.

____

The vase is red.

____

The volcano is hot.

____

Ww

Walrus

____

Whale

____

Watermelon

____

The walrus has tusk.

____

The whale lives in the ocean.

____

The watermelon is juicy.

____

Xx

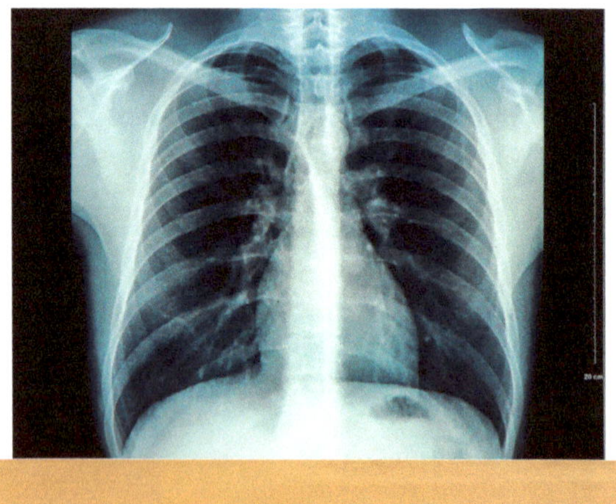

Xray

____

Xylophone

____

X-mas Tree

____

The doctor took some X-rays.

____

I play the Xylophone.

____

The X-mas Tree is big and green.

____

Yy________

Yo-yo

____

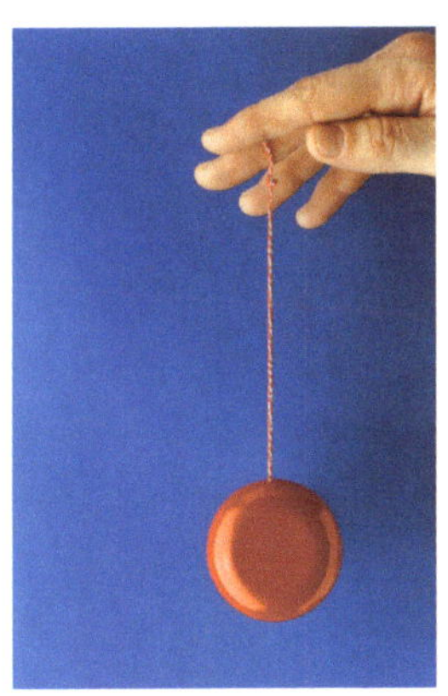

Yak

____

Yarn

____

The yo-yo is fun to play with.
____

The yak has big horns.
____

I can knitt a sweater with yarn.

____

Zz____________

Zebra

____

Zoo

____

Zero

____

The zebra has black stripes.

____

The zoo has a lot of animals.

____

There are zero dollars.

____